LAND THAT I LOVE
Regions of the United States

THE MID-ATLANTIC

Niccole Bartley

PowerKiDS press.
New York

Published in 2015 by The Rosen Publishing Group, Inc.
29 East 21st Street, New York, NY 10010

First Edition

Editor: Joanne Randolph
Photo Research: Katie Stryker
Book Design: Colleen Bialecki

Photo Credits: Cover, p. 5 Orhan Cam/Shutterstock.com; p. 4 Rene Pi/Shutterstock.com; p. 6 Universal Image Group/ Contributor/Getty Images; p. 7 MyLoupe/Contributor/Universal Images Group/Getty Images; p. 8 Stock Montage/Contributor/ Archive Photos/Getty Images; p. 9 Popperfoto/Contributor/Getty Images; p. 10 Kean Collection/Archive Photos/Getty Images; p. 11 Buyenlarge/Contributor/Archive Photos/Getty Images; pp. 12, 16 (top) m-kojot/iStock/Thinkstock; pp. 13, 23 Jon Bilous/Shutterstock.com; p. 15 AndresGarciaM/iStock/Thinkstock; p. 16 (bottom left) Todd Taulman/Shutterstock.com; p. 16 (bottom right) Matt McClain/Shutterstock.com p. 17 (inset) S. Borisov/Shutterstock.com; p. 17 (bottom) Albert de Brujin/ Thinkstock; p. 17 (center) trekandshoot/Shutterstock.com; p. 18 Critterbiz/Shutterstock; p. 19 (top) 4736202690/ Shutterstock.com; p. 19 (bottom) Lissandra Melo/Shutterstock.com; p. 20 Dervin Witmer/Shutterstock.com; p. 21 Wade H. Massie/Shutterstock.com; p. 21 spirit of america/Shutterstock.com; p. 22 Cathlyn Melloam/Photodisc/Getty Images; p. 24 ruigsantos/Shutterstock.com; p. 25 (bottom) Vlad G/Shutterstock.com; p. 25 (top) John Greim/Getty Images; p. 26 Huw Jones/Lonely Planet Images/Getty Images; p. 27 Jorg Hackermann/Shutterstock.com; p. 28 Dennis Drenner/Getty Images; p. 29 Danita Delimont/Gallo Images/Getty Images; pp. 30, 17 (top) dell640/iStock/Thinkstock.

Library of Congress Cataloging-in-Publication Data

Bartley, Niccole.
The Mid-Atlantic / by Niccole Bartley. — 1st ed.
    pages cm. — (Land that I love: regions of the United States)
Includes index.
ISBN 978-1-4777-6855-6 (library binding) — ISBN 978-1-4777-6853-2 (paperback) —
ISBN 978-1-4777-6635-4 (6-pack)
1. Middle Atlantic States—Juvenile literature. I. Title.
F106.B375 2015
974—dc23
                        2014000411

Manufactured in the United States of America

CPSIA Compliance Information: Batch #WS14PK9: For Further Information contact Rosen Publishing, New York, New York at 1-800-237-9932

CONTENTS

THE MID-ATLANTIC REGION

The mid-Atlantic **region** is just south of New England. The mid-Atlantic states are New York, New Jersey, Pennsylvania, Delaware, Maryland, Virginia, and West Virginia. There are many important cities in the mid-Atlantic region, and many people live and work there. It is a busy region!

One of the most famous mid-Atlantic cities is New York City. When many people think of New York, they picture the island of Manhattan, shown here. Manhattan is one of New York's five boroughs, or sections.

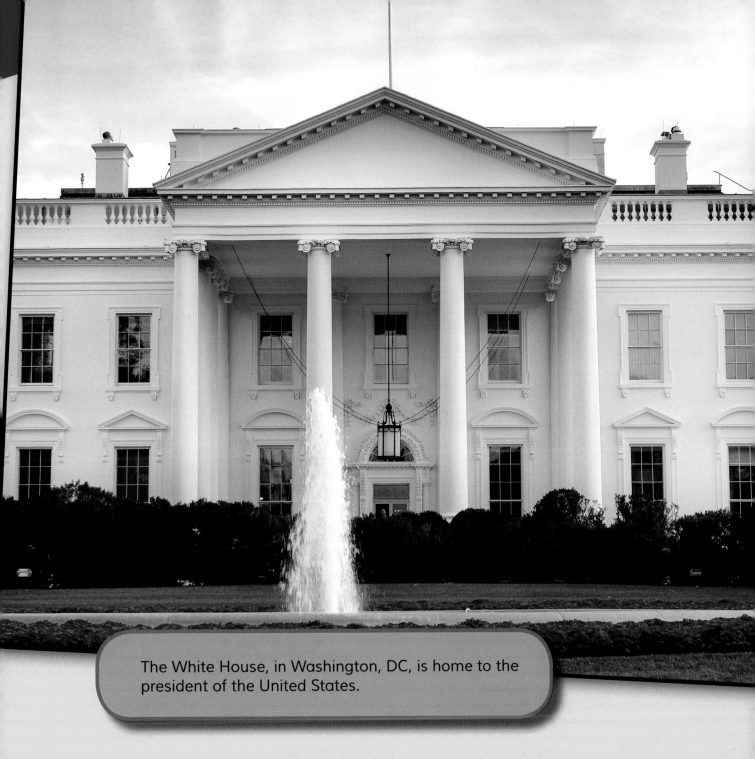

The White House, in Washington, DC, is home to the president of the United States.

New York City and Washington, DC, are in the mid-Atlantic region. New York City is one of the largest and most important cities in the world. Washington, DC, also known as the District of Columbia, is the capital of the United States. The Mid-Atlantic has played an important role in the development of American culture and **industry**.

Native Americans called the Lenapes were among the first humans to live in the mid-Atlantic region. The Iroquois were another powerful group of Native Americans living in present-day New York State.

The Lenapes and Iroquois lived in a similar way. The men hunted and fished, and the women were farmers. The women also did the cooking and took care of the children. They lived in villages of **wigwams** and **longhouses**. They wore deerskin clothing and moccasins.

Here William Penn is making a treaty, or agreement, with the Lenape Indians in Pennsylvania. You can see the clothing styles of the Lenapes here.

This longhouse on the Delaware River was built to show what a typical Lenape longhouse looked like.

Disease brought by the British settlers and later war with the Americans forced the Lenapes and Iroquois out of their original homeland in the mid-Atlantic region. The remaining Lenapes today live mostly in Oklahoma and Canada. The remaining Iroquois people are in Canada.

THE THREE SISTERS OF THE LENAPES

The Lenape women practiced a type of farming called companion planting. This means that they planted certain plants next to each other because they grow well together. The most famous group of plants used in companion planting was called the Three Sisters. The Three Sisters were generally corn, beans, and squash. The corn stalks grow tall and strong and support the growing bean vines. The squash plants have large leaves that cover the ground and provide shade and mulch for the corn and beans. Many farmers and gardeners still use this technique today!

The Lenape Indians met the first European **explorers** in canoes in New York Harbor in 1524. Giovanni Verrazano led these explorers. He was the first of many European explorers to visit the region. In 1607, the English **founded** Jamestown, Virginia. Jamestown was the first permanent English colony in North America. In 1614, the Dutch created a fur-trading post in Albany in present-day New York State.

The Declaration of Independence was written and signed in Independence Hall, in Philadelphia, in 1776. The US Constitution was also drafted and signed in the hall in 1787.

Most of the battles of the American Revolution were fought in New York and New Jersey. The Colonial troops were led by George Washington. Here he is shown crossing the Delaware River to surprise Hessian troops at Trenton, New Jersey.

The early settlers who arrived in the 1700s were mostly farmers, traders, and fishermen. Dutch settlers moved into the Hudson River valley in what is now New York State. Settlers from Sweden went to Delaware. English settlers founded Maryland and Pennsylvania. All of the settlers came to America seeking religious freedom and a new way of life.

Many **immigrants** continued to arrive in the mid-Atlantic states through the 1800s and 1900s. They have greatly shaped the region. The mid-Atlantic region is often thought of as the first true example of the **melting-pot** society found in the modern United States.

The Erie Canal was originally about 363 miles (584 km) long and provided a shipping route between Albany and Buffalo, New York. It opened in 1825.

During the Industrial Revolution, many factories were built in the mid-Atlantic region and elsewhere in the United States. Immigrants and children often worked in these factories under harsh and dangerous conditions.

Cities grew quickly along major ports and waterways. New York City is located on the Hudson River, Philadelphia is on the Delaware River, and Baltimore is on Chesapeake Bay. The region's location in the middle of the 13 colonies made it the heart of the young country.

WRITE ABOUT IT!

During the Industrial Revolution, many railroads and canals were built to make shipping goods and people easier. Do some research on the history of the Erie Canal. Write an expository paragraph on how the canal changed life in New York.

MOUNTAINS, SWAMPS, AND WATERFALLS

The Mid-Atlantic is one of the most heavily populated regions in the country. Much of that population is located in the **urban** areas in the northeastern part of the region. The rest of the region is more lightly populated and has beautiful natural features.

Long ago, glaciers traveled through the region and left many mountains and river valleys. The Adirondacks, in New York, and the Allegheny Mountains, in Pennsylvania, Maryland, Virginia, and West Virginia, are part of the Appalachian Mountains. The Hudson and Delaware River valleys have rich, fertile soil, making the region good for farming.

Niagara Falls is made up of three waterfalls on the border between New York and Canada. The falls have a vertical drop of 165 feet (50 m).

Shenandoah Mountain is a mountain ridge known for its red spruce forest. The name Shenandoah comes from the Iroquoian word for "deer," which are also plentiful there. The ridge stretches from West Virginia into Virginia.

There are famous swamps in southeastern Virginia and amazing spruce-fir forests in northern Pennsylvania. There are hundreds of waterfalls in New York, New Jersey, Pennsylvania, and Maryland.

THE MAID OF THE MIST: A NATIVE AMERICAN LEGEND

The Ongiaras, a Native American tribe, lived near Niagara Falls, in present-day Niagara, New York. There is a legend about an Indian maiden who lives in the mist of the falls. She was saved from death by the god of thunder, Heno, who lived in Niagara Falls. After her rescue, she lived with Heno and his sons.

Soon after the maiden went to live with Heno, the Ongiaras began to get sick and die. A great snake was poisoning the waters. Heno let the maiden warn her people about the evil snake. She told them to move to a location on higher ground until the snake was gone.

In a few days, the snake returned to the village. Heno threw a thunderbolt at the creature and killed it. Heno and the maiden had saved the Ongiaras. You can still hear the thunder of Heno in Niagara Falls.

The Gateway to the United States

Since the earliest European settlers arrived, people have continued to flow into the United States seeking better lives. In the late 1800s, an immigration station was built on Ellis Island. This small island is in Upper New York Bay, just south of Manhattan and near the Statue of Liberty. It was built as a place for European immigrants to enter the United States after the long voyage across the Atlantic Ocean.

More than 12 million immigrants passed through Ellis Island between 1892 until it closed, in 1954. Immigrants left Ellis Island and settled in towns and cities all over the country. Today, more than 100 million Americans have **ancestors** who first arrived at Ellis Island. This is more than 30 percent of the population.

Immigrants who were approved to enter the United States spent from 2 to 5 hours at Ellis Island. Arrivals were asked 29 questions, including their names, occupations, and the amount of money they carried. Today Ellis Island is a museum.

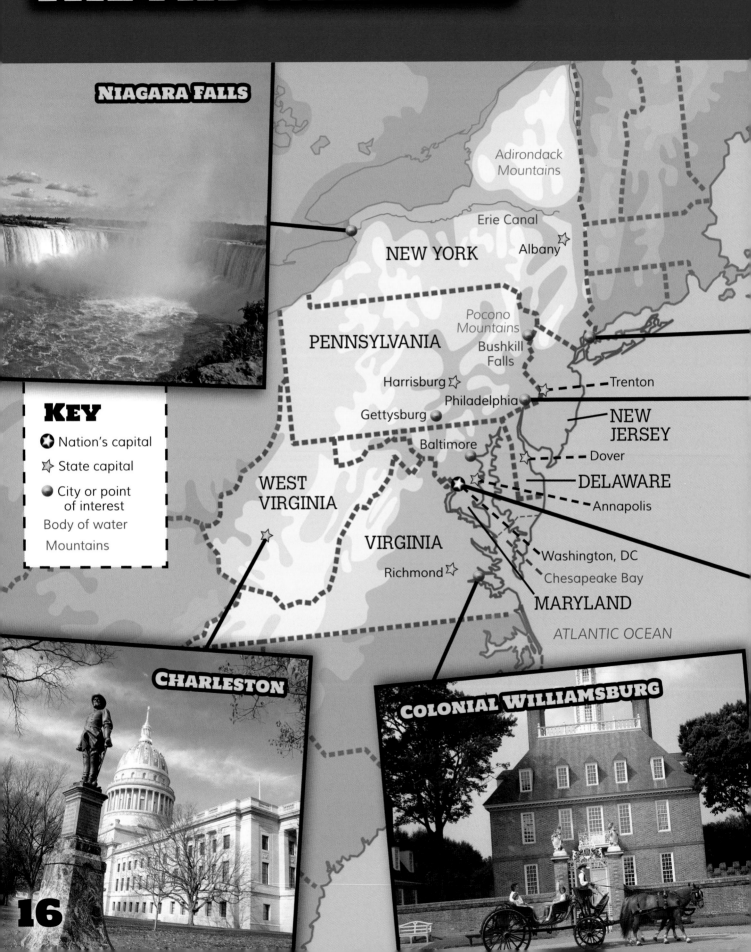

THE MID-ATLANTIC

NIAGARA FALLS

KEY

✪ Nation's capital

☆ State capital

● City or point of interest

Body of water

Mountains

Adirondack Mountains

Erie Canal

NEW YORK

☆ Albany

Pocono Mountains

PENNSYLVANIA

Bushkill Falls

Harrisburg ☆

Philadelphia

Gettysburg

─ Trenton

NEW JERSEY

Baltimore

☆ ─ ─ Dover

DELAWARE

WEST VIRGINIA

─ Annapolis

VIRGINIA

Washington, DC

Richmond ☆

Chesapeake Bay

MARYLAND

ATLANTIC OCEAN

CHARLESTON

COLONIAL WILLIAMSBURG

NEW YORK CITY

STATUE OF LIBERTY

INDEPENDENCE HALL

WHITE HOUSE, WASHINGTON, DC

The Mid-Atlantic is one of the most developed and highly populated regions in the United States. Small birds and mammals, such as squirrels, deer, rabbits, hawks, and robins, are still found in the **suburban** and urban areas. They have adapted well to living in these highly populated areas. Larger animals do not have enough habitat space in these developed areas, though.

Black bears make their homes in the mountains and forests of the mid-Atlantic region. They live in many other places in the United States, too.

Maryland is famous for its crabs, which are plentiful in Chesapeake Bay.

Washington, DC, is known for its cherry trees. Hundreds of people come to the capital each spring for the National Cherry Blossom Festival.

To see larger mammals, such as bears and moose, one must head to less populated areas or national parks that have been set aside for plants and animals. The more **rural** areas of upstate New York, Virginia, and West Virginia still have a greater **diversity** of wildlife.

NATURAL RESOURCES AND INDUSTRY

The most important **natural resource** of the mid-Atlantic region is its location on the Atlantic seaboard and all of the waterways that connect it to the rest of the country. Because of the rich soil and access to water, the early settlers were mostly farmers, traders, and fishermen.

By the 1800s, the mid-Atlantic states became the center of heavy industry. Much of the nation's iron, glass, and steel were produced in this region. Many mid-Atlantic cities became shipping ports, including New York and Philadelphia, which were major commerce centers.

Pennsylvania's Quakers and Amish became skilled farmers when they settled in the region. Today, many still run successful farms. This is an Amish dairy farm in Lancaster County, Pennsylvania.

Tourism is a major industry in Williamsburg, Virginia. Hundreds of people visit Colonial Williamsburg to learn about what life was like in Colonial America.

New York is still the nation's largest city and its financial and cultural capital. Today, the most important industries in the region are finance, drug manufacturing, technology, education, and communications.

This is an old steel mill in Pittsburgh, Pennsylvania. Steel production is no longer Pittsburgh's main industry, though, as the city has become a leader in technology and finance.

MID-ATLANTIC CITIES

The mid-Atlantic region is home to many large cities, including coastal port cities such as New York City, Newark, Philadelphia, Washington, DC, and Baltimore. There are also interior cities, such as Pittsburgh, Pennsylvania, and Albany and Buffalo, in New York State. These cities help make the mid-Atlantic region one of the most urban and wealthy regions in the nation. The cities are not only home to many businesses, but they also have many restaurants, museums, universities, and historic sites.

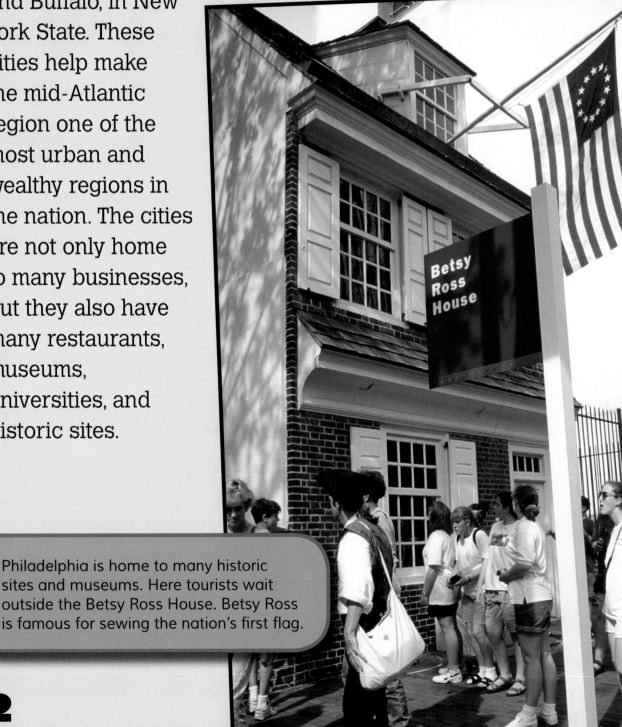

Philadelphia is home to many historic sites and museums. Here tourists wait outside the Betsy Ross House. Betsy Ross is famous for sewing the nation's first flag.

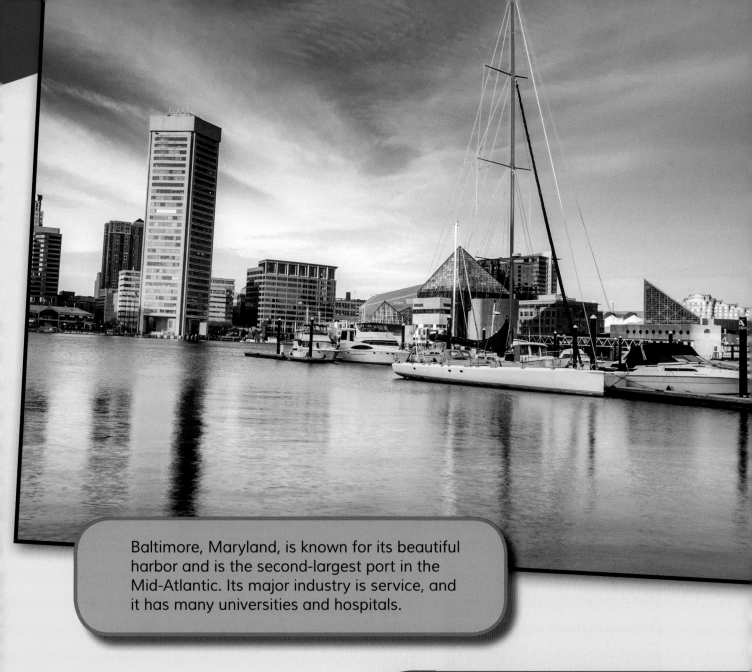

Baltimore, Maryland, is known for its beautiful harbor and is the second-largest port in the Mid-Atlantic. Its major industry is service, and it has many universities and hospitals.

The cities in the mid-Atlantic region together make it one of the most important centers of finance, media, communications, education, medicine, and technology in the world.

THE UNITED NATIONS

New York City is home to the United Nations. The United Nations is an international organization with 193 member countries. Its main job is to get countries to work together and prevent war.

The mid-Atlantic region is home to many famous man-made landmarks and historic sites. In New York City, there are hundreds of famous landmarks and tourist sites. Some of the most important historical sites in New York are the Statue of Liberty, the Empire State Building, and Ellis Island.

In Washington, DC, tourists get to witness the nation's government in action when they visit the White House, the Capitol, and the Supreme Court Building. The Smithsonian, the world's largest complex of museums, is also in DC.

Thousands of people visit the top of the Empire State Building, in New York. It offers amazing views of the city and once was the tallest building in the world.

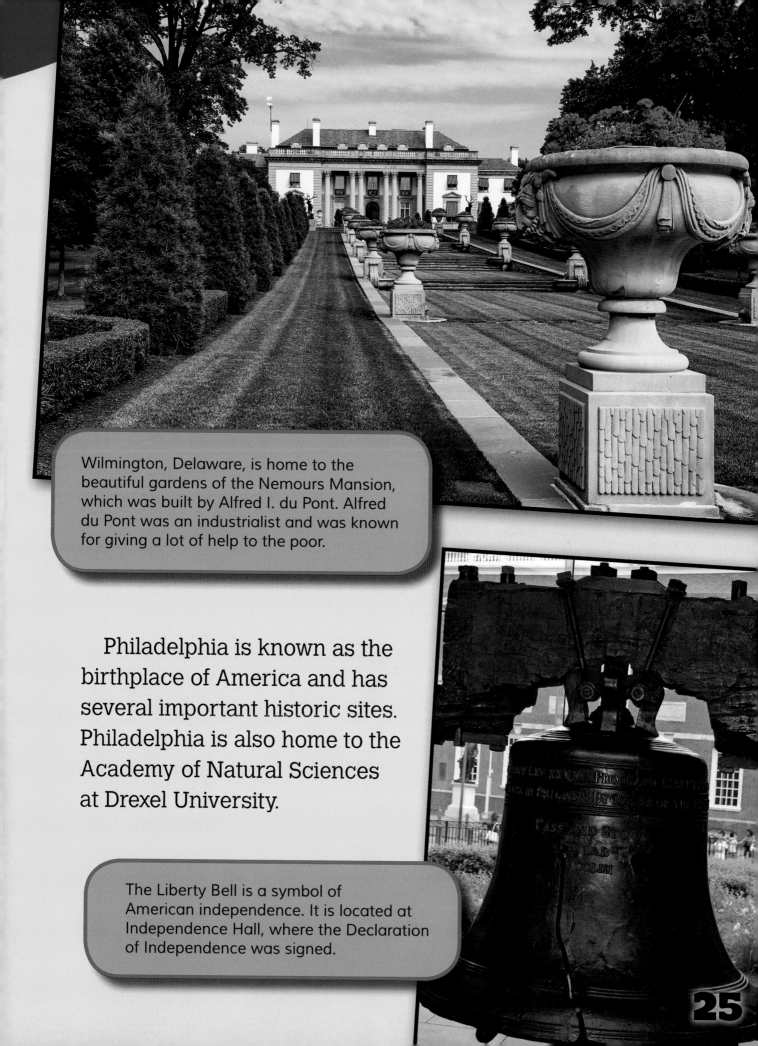

Wilmington, Delaware, is home to the beautiful gardens of the Nemours Mansion, which was built by Alfred I. du Pont. Alfred du Pont was an industrialist and was known for giving a lot of help to the poor.

Philadelphia is known as the birthplace of America and has several important historic sites. Philadelphia is also home to the Academy of Natural Sciences at Drexel University.

The Liberty Bell is a symbol of American independence. It is located at Independence Hall, where the Declaration of Independence was signed.

MID-ATLANTIC CULTURE

The culture of the mid-Atlantic region is very typical of American culture. For 300 years, immigrants came to the region in search of religious freedom and a new life. As a result, the people in the Mid-Atlantic tend to be tolerant and open-minded and come from many different backgrounds and religions.

Street festivals are common in New York City. A street is blocked off so that people may walk in the street, shop at vendors, and try local and ethnic foods.

Thousands of people visit the museums in Washington, DC, each year. This is the National Air and Space Museum.

The early settlers were mostly English, Swedish, and Dutch farmers. They created the rural culture that still exists in places like western Pennsylvania, upstate New York, and southern Virginia.

Many German, Jewish, Polish, Irish, and Italian immigrants settled in the mid-Atlantic states in the 1800s, especially in the urban areas. After the Civil War, many freed African-American slaves moved North to the urban areas also. They all brought their own traditions and made new cuisines popular in the region.

Nothing has changed the culture of the mid-Atlantic region more than the rise of the suburbs. A suburb is a community outside of a larger city. The explosion of people living in suburbs in the Mid-Atlantic was led by cheaper automobiles and improvements in public transportation. This meant Americans could now live farther away from their workplaces.

Seafood is a big part of many Marylanders' lives. Many people there catch fish, shellfish, and crabs for a living. Tourists and residents alike enjoy visiting Maryland's restaurants to enjoy fresh-caught seafood.

It is not uncommon to see families in horse-drawn carriages in Pennsylvania. The Amish people who make their homes there practice a simple way of life and do not use modern technology.

Downtown areas became places where companies were located, and the suburbs became the places where most people slept and lived. The mid-Atlantic region is today the most suburbanized region in the nation.

WRITE ABOUT IT!

Pretend you and your family take a trip to one of the cities in the Mid-Atlantic. Write a letter or postcard home to a friend or relative telling him or her about your trip! Be sure to research some of the important landmarks and tourist spots to visit in your city. Write about what new foods you will try, where you will sleep, and what you might do!

A FAST-PACED REGION

The mid-Atlantic region is a fast-paced place to live and work! The region is home to many different groups of people. There are many big cities, such as New York, Washington, DC, Philadelphia, and Baltimore, in the region. These cities have led the nation in finance, arts, and culture for the past 300 years and will continue to do so in the future! Many people live, work, and visit the Mid-Atlantic and enjoy all of the rich culture and history that make this place so special.

New York City is just one of the mid-Atlantic region's major urban centers.

GLOSSARY

ancestors (AN-ses-terz) Relatives who lived long ago.

disease (dih-ZEEZ) An illness or sickness.

diversity (duh-VER-suh-tee) Having a lot of difference and variety.

explorers (ek-SPLOR-erz) People who travel and look for new land.

founded (FOWN-did) Started.

immigrants (IH-muh-grunts) People who move to a new country from another country.

industry (IN-dus-tree) A business in which many people work and make money producing something.

longhouses (LONG-how-zez) Long Native American shelters.

melting pot (MELT-ing-PAHT) Having to do with a place with people of a lot of different races and cultures.

natural resource (NA-chuh-rul REE-sors) Something in nature that can be used by people.

region (REE-jun) A different part of Earth.

rural (RUR-ul) In the country or in a farming area.

suburban (suh-BER-bun) Having to do with an area of homes and businesses that is near a large city.

urban (UR-bun) Having to do with a city.

wigwams (WIG-wahmz) Domed Native American shelters.

INDEX

WEBSITES

Due to the changing nature of Internet links, PowerKids Press has developed an online list of websites related to the subject of this book. This site is updated regularly. Please use this link to access the list:

www.powerkidslinks.com/ltil/mida/